What's the Issue?

WHAT'S FREEDOM OF RELIGION?

By Joseph Stanley

KidHaven
PUBLISHING

Published in 2019 by
KidHaven Publishing, an Imprint of Greenhaven Publishing, LLC
353 3rd Avenue
Suite 255
New York, NY 10010

Designer: Andrea Davison-Bartolotta
Editor: Katie Kawa

Photo credits: Cover (top) Brian A. Jackson/Shutterstock.com; cover (bottom) Kristina Sophie/Shutterstock.com; p. 4 James R. Martin/Shutterstock.com; p. 5 (top right) Amir Bajrich/Shutterstock.com; p. 5 (bottom left) Golden Pixels LLC/Shutterstock.com; p. 5 (top left) Monkey Business Images/Shutterstock.com; p. 5 (bottom right) SantiPhotoSS/Shutterstock.com; p. 6 GeorgiosArt/iStock/Thinkstock; p. 7 (main) courtesy of the National Archives; pp. 7, 21 (background) didecs/iStock/Thinkstock; p. 8 Everett Historical/Shutterstock.com; p. 9 KAREN BLEIER/AFP/Getty Images; p. 11 (background) jakkapan21/iStock/Thinkstock; p. 11 (Hindu) India Picture/Shutterstock.com; p. 11 (Muslim) michaeljung/Shutterstock.com; p. 11 (Jewish) Africa Studio/Shutterstock.com; p. 11 (Christian) CartoonMini/Shutterstock.com; p. 11 (Buddhist) szefei/Shutterstock.com; p. 13 Kdonmuang/Shutterstock.com; p. 14 Michele Eve Sandberg/Corbis via Getty Images; p. 15 Robert Nickelsberg/Getty Images; p. 17 SAUL LOEB/AFP/Getty Images; p. 19 sirtravelalot/Shutterstock.com; p. 20 GagliardiImages/Shutterstock.com.

Cataloging-in-Publication Data

Names: Stanley, Joseph.
Title: What's freedom of religion? / Joseph Stanley.
Description: New York : KidHaven Publishing, 2019. | Series: What's the issue? | Includes glossary and index.
Identifiers: ISBN 9781534527935 (pbk.) | ISBN 9781534527959 (library bound) | ISBN 9781534527942 (6 pack) | ISBN 9781534528086 (ebook)
Subjects: LCSH: United States. Constitution. 1st Amendment–Juvenile literature. | Freedom of religion–United States–Juvenile literature.
Classification: LCC KF4770.S763 2019 | DDC 342.7308'53–dc23

Printed in the United States of America

CPSIA compliance Information: Batch #BW19KL: For further information contact Greenhaven Publishing LLC, New York, New York at 1-844-317-7404.

Please visit our website, www.greenhavenpublishing.com. For a free color catalog of all our high-quality books, call toll free 1-844-317-7404 or fax 1-844-317-7405.

CONTENTS

A Free Country

People often call the United States a free country. This means that people living there have many freedoms, including freedom of speech and freedom of the press. People can freely gather in peaceful groups and freely ask the government for things they need.

People can also freely practice different religions, or belief systems. These can include a belief in God, a belief in many gods, or a belief in nothing at all. Freedom of religion is an important part of life in the United States, and Americans often feel very strongly about it.

Facing the Facts

A major study of religious beliefs in the United States was done in 2014. That study showed that 53 percent of American adults view religion as very important to them.

People in the United States are free to practice whatever religion they choose—or no religion at all.

The Bill of Rights

Freedom of religion is part of the U.S. Constitution, which set up how the U.S. government is run. It wasn't part of the Constitution from the very beginning, but it was included as one of the first ten amendments, or changes, to the document. These amendments were put together in what is known as the Bill of Rights.

The Bill of Rights **protects** many freedoms that are valued in the United States. Freedom of religion is protected under the First Amendment. The other First Amendment freedoms are freedom of speech, freedom of the press, freedom to **assemble** peacefully, and freedom to **petition** the government.

James Madison, author of the Bill of Rights

Facing the Facts

The Bill of Rights was ratified, or formally approved, in 1791.

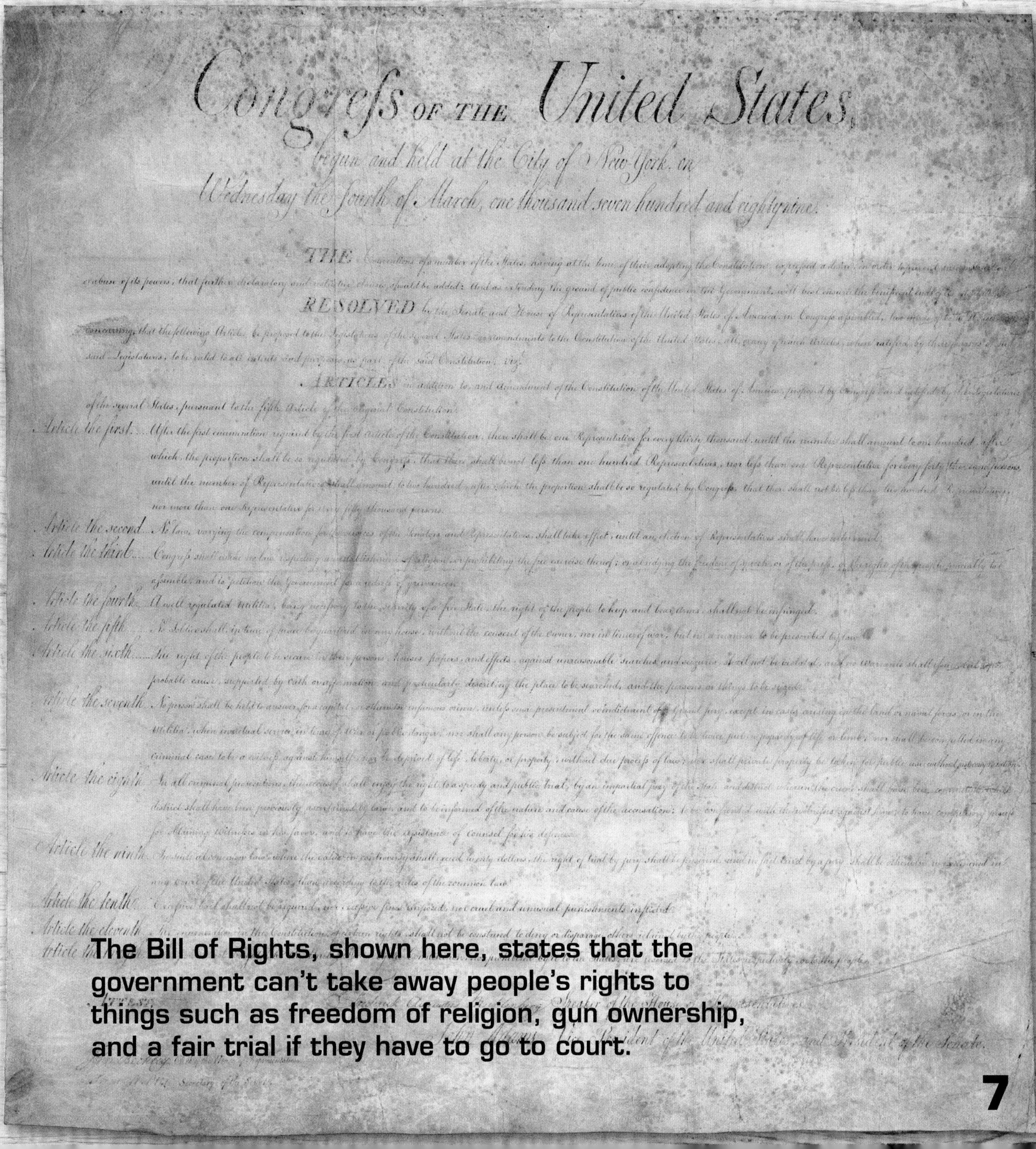
Congress of the United States,
begun and held at the City of New-York, on
Wednesday the fourth of March, one thousand seven hundred and eighty nine.

The Bill of Rights, shown here, states that the government can't take away people's rights to things such as freedom of religion, gun ownership, and a fair trial if they have to go to court.

Staying Separate

What does freedom of religion really mean in the United States? The answer is found in two clauses, or parts, of the First Amendment that help explain it more clearly. The first clause explains that the U.S. government can't establish, or set up, an official religion for the whole country to follow. This is why it's called the Establishment Clause.

This clause also keeps the government from acting in a way that favors a certain religion over others. The government can't control religious groups, and religious groups can't control the government. This is known as the separation of church and state.

Facing the Facts

In 1802, President Thomas Jefferson wrote that the Establishment Clause would put up a "wall of separation" between church and state.

Many people have strong feelings about the separation of church and state. They believe freedom of religion can only be protected if the two stay separate.

Free to Express Your Faith

The second clause that deals with religious freedom is known as the Free Exercise Clause. It states that the U.S. government can't keep people from freely exercising, or practicing, their religious beliefs.

Many different religions are practiced in the United States, and they're all practiced in different ways. Some require special clothing, while others require prayer at certain times. The Free Exercise Clause states that the government can't keep people from wearing clothes, celebrating holidays, or doing anything else that expresses, or shows, their religious beliefs as long as they're not harming anyone.

Facing the Facts

As of 2014, 22.8 percent of Americans said they don't belong to any **organized** religion.

These are just some of the different religious groups Americans belong to. Other Americans don't have any religious beliefs. The First Amendment protects all of these Americans—not just members of one group.

religious groups in the United States

Christian

- Protestant
- Catholic
- Mormon

Jewish

Muslim

Buddhist

Hindu

Freedom of Religion Around the World

Freedom of religion is a part of life in the United States, but people in many other countries don't have that same freedom. As of 2015, more than 80 countries either unofficially favor one religion over others or have an official national religion. One example is Iran, where Islam is the official religion.

In some cases, governments use laws and other actions to control members of some religious groups. People can go to jail in some countries for not following the official religion. In other countries, they can be **punished** for expressing any religious belief.

Facing the Facts

A 2015 study of 198 countries showed that governments used force against religious groups in 23 of those countries.

Some Muslim women, or women who practice Islam, choose to wear a head covering called a hijab, but they're forced to wear them in Iran. In other countries, people have tried to force Muslim women to take off their hijab. Women don't feel free to express their beliefs in either example.

Fear or Freedom?

Even in the United States, people don't always feel free to practice their chosen religion. Most Americans believe people of all religions should be able to freely express their religious beliefs. However, some Americans disagree. They believe people with certain religious beliefs should be treated differently—or not allowed in the United States at all.

People who practice Islam are sometimes the **victims** of this kind of intolerance, or lack of acceptance. Some Jewish people are attacked for their beliefs, too. Americans who support religious freedom for everyone often speak out against this poor treatment and work to help people of all religions feel safe.

Facing the Facts

As of 2016, Jewish people were attacked more often for their beliefs than members of any other religious group in the United States. Unkind treatment of Jewish people is known as anti-Semitism.

Some people who claim to practice Islam have carried out **terrorist** attacks around the world. This has led to an increase in Islamophobia, or fear and dislike of all Muslims. However, many people understand that the actions of a few bad people shouldn't **affect** how all people who practice a religion are treated.

Different Points of View

In a country with many different belief systems, **debates** about religion and how it's practiced are common. In the United States, people sometimes argue that the idea of the separation of church and state gets in the way of their religious freedom.

Issues such as same-sex marriage and health care are at the center of many debates about religious freedom. Some people believe honoring same-sex marriages or paying for some health care services goes against their religious beliefs. Others believe these aren't religious issues. It's up to the U.S. Supreme Court to decide cases about religious freedom and how it applies to life in the United States today.

Facing the Facts

In a 2015 poll, 54 percent of Americans who were asked said they think it's wrong for a business to refuse to serve someone because it goes against their religious beliefs.

Freedom of religion was written into the Constitution hundreds of years ago, but it's still a major part of life in the United States. People have debated issues such as the separation of church and state since the United States was founded, and they continue to do so today.

Celebrating Diversity

Debates about religious freedom can cause hurt feelings. However, when they're handled in a respectful way, many people believe they make countries such as the United States stronger.

Freedom of religion is part of what makes the United States such a diverse country, which means it's filled with many different kinds of people. Although most Americans are Christians, people of all religions—and people who don't practice any religion—are welcome. When people with different religious beliefs freely and respectfully share those beliefs with each other, they learn important new things about the world and the people around them.

Religious diversity is one of many kinds of diversity celebrated in the United States. No two Americans are exactly alike!

Facing the Facts

A 2015 study showed that 66 percent of older Americans believe being Christian is an important part of being American, but only 35 percent of young adults share that belief.

Respecting All Religions

Religion is generally considered a very personal part of someone's life. A person's beliefs are often very important to them, and they should be treated with respect. This is why religious freedom is valued in countries such as the United States. It helps make sure that all people—no matter their beliefs—are treated equally. It also protects the diversity that makes America special.

Sometimes it can be hard to understand why people from different religious groups believe what they do. However, freedom of religion means that everyone has the right to their own beliefs and to practice those beliefs without fear.

WHAT CAN YOU DO?

Learn about different religions and belief systems.

Raise money for groups that protect religious freedom in the United States and around the world.

Treat people with kindness no matter what their religious beliefs are.

Think about your own religious beliefs and talk about them with your parents or guardians.

Listen respectfully to others when they talk about their religious beliefs.

How can you help make sure all people can freely express their beliefs? It starts with showing others respect and kindness.

Facing the Facts

In U.S. public schools, religion classes and organized prayer aren't allowed because of the First Amendment. However, students can pray or express their religious beliefs on their own as long as they don't get in the way of other students' learning.

GLOSSARY

affect: To produce an effect on something.

assemble: To meet together in one place.

debate: An argument or discussion about an issue, generally between two sides. Also, to take part in such an argument or discussion.

organized: Set up in a formal way with leaders and rules for doing things.

petition: To make a request.

protect: To keep safe.

punish: To make someone suffer for doing something wrong.

terrorist: Having to do with the use of violence and fear as a way to achieve a political goal.

victim: A person who is hurt by someone else.

FOR MORE INFORMATION

WEBSITES

America's Founding Documents: The Bill of Rights

www.archives.gov/founding-docs/bill-of-rights

This U.S. government website features facts about the Bill of Rights and pictures of the document.

URI Kids: World Religions

uri.org/kids/world-religions

This website explains basic points about religion to young people and features facts about different belief systems to help spread tolerance and respect for all religious groups.

BOOKS

Bullard, Lisa. *My Religion, Your Religion.* Minneapolis, MN: Millbrook Press, 2015.

Hoover, Stephanie. *Freedom of Religion.* New York, NY: Gareth Stevens Publishing, 2017.

Knight, Khadijah. *My Muslim Faith.* London, UK: Cherrytree Books, 2016.

INDEX